Senses

Library Edition Published 1991

Published by Marshall Cavendish Corporation
2415 Jerusalem Avenue
PO Box 587
North Bellmore
NY 11710

Printed in Italy by New Interlitho, Milan

Library edition produced by Pemberton Press Limited

Library of Congress Cataloging-in-Data applied for.

ISBN 1 85435 268 7 (set)
ISBN 1 85435 271 7

SECRETS OF SCIENCE
Senses

Robin Kerrod and Susan Baker

Illustrated by Mike Atkinson

Safety First

☐ Ask your parents or another adult before you start any experiment, especially if you are using matches or anything hot, sharp or poisonous.

☐ Don't wear your best clothes. Wear old ones or an overall.

☐ If you work on a table, use an old one and protect it with paper or cardboard.

☐ Do water experiments in the sink or outdoors.

☐ Strike matches away from your body and make sure they are out before you throw them away.

☐ Make sure candles are standing securely.

☐ Wear oven gloves when handling anything hot.

☐ Take care when cutting things. Always cut away from your body.

☐ Don't use cans with jagged edges. Use ones with lids.

☐ Use only non-toxic white glue, glue sticks or paste.

☐ Never taste chemicals, unless the book tells you to.

☐ Label all bottles and jars containing chemicals, and store them where young children can't get at them – and not in the family food cupboard.

☐ Never use or play with household electricity. It can KILL. Use a flashlight or lantern battery.

☐ When you have finished an experiment, put your things away, clean up and wash your hands.

Contents

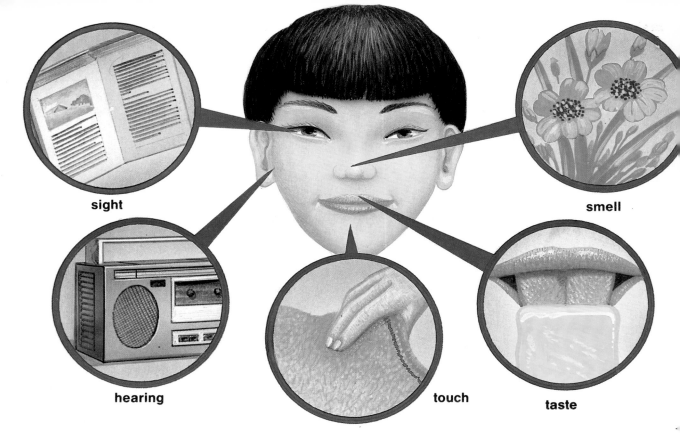

sight

smell

hearing

touch

taste

Sensational Senses

Our bodies have five different senses that help us find out about the world around us. They are sight, hearing, smell, taste and touch.

You see with your eyes. You hear with your ears. You smell with your nose. You taste with your tongue. You feel with your skin. Your eyes, ears, nose, tongue and skin are called sense organs.

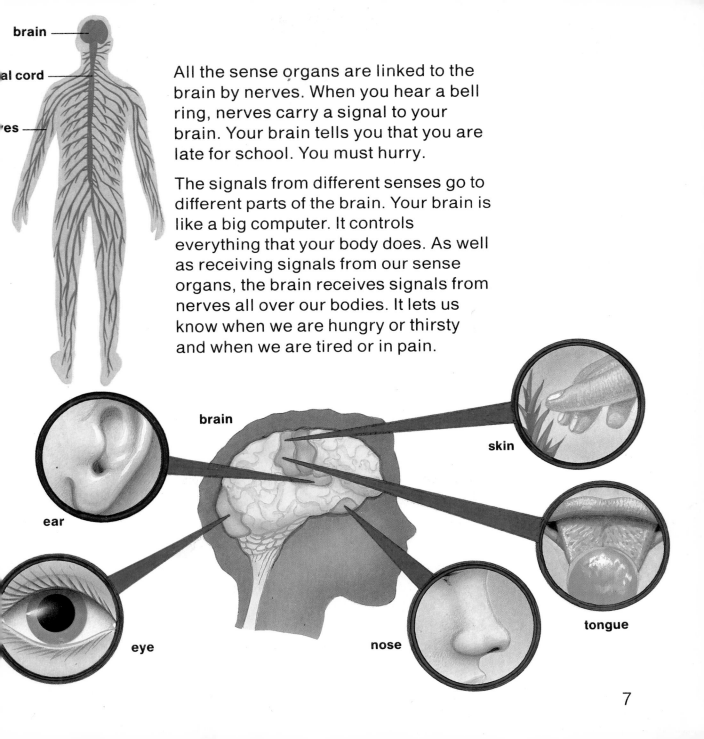

brain

al cord

es

All the sense organs are linked to the brain by nerves. When you hear a bell ring, nerves carry a signal to your brain. Your brain tells you that you are late for school. You must hurry.

The signals from different senses go to different parts of the brain. Your brain is like a big computer. It controls everything that your body does. As well as receiving signals from our sense organs, the brain receives signals from nerves all over our bodies. It lets us know when we are hungry or thirsty and when we are tired or in pain.

brain

skin

ear

tongue

eye

nose

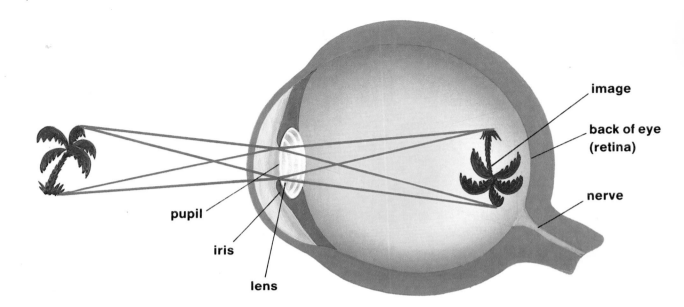

Bright Eyes

Look at your eyes in a mirror. In the center of each eye there is a black circle called a pupil. It is a hole that lets light into the eye.

Behind the pupil is a lens. Light from the object you are looking at passes through the lens. It throws a tiny, upside-down picture of the object on the back of the eye. A nerve carries signals to the brain that tell it the color and shape of the picture. The brain turns the picture the right way up and you see the object.

The colored part of your eye is called the iris. It is a ring of muscle that makes the pupil larger or smaller. In bright light the pupil gets smaller. In low light it gets larger to let more light into the eye. See this for yourself, with a mirror and a lamp. Do your pupils get smaller when you switch the lamp on?

Light is made of all the colors of the rainbow. Our eyes can see color only in bright light. Switch off the main light in a room at night. What can you see? Can you see any colors?

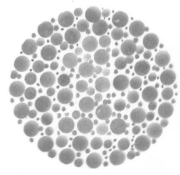

Some people confuse certain colors. They are color blind. If you can see a 1 in the circle, you are not color blind

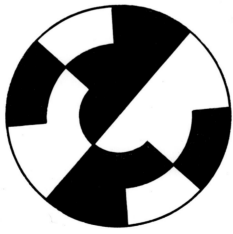

Make a Rainbow Spinner

1 You need a circle of white card, black paint or a felt tip pen, and a cocktail stick.

2 Copy the pattern exactly. It must be really black not gray.

3 Push the cocktail stick through the center and spin your top. What do you see?

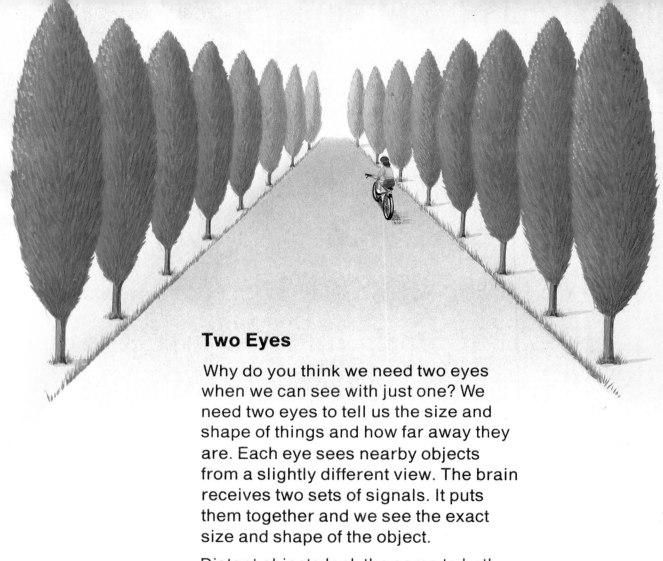

Two Eyes

Why do you think we need two eyes when we can see with just one? We need two eyes to tell us the size and shape of things and how far away they are. Each eye sees nearby objects from a slightly different view. The brain receives two sets of signals. It puts them together and we see the exact size and shape of the object.

Distant objects look the same to both eyes. If you look at a long straight road, the sides of the road seem to disappear in the distance.
Some people's eyes do not work

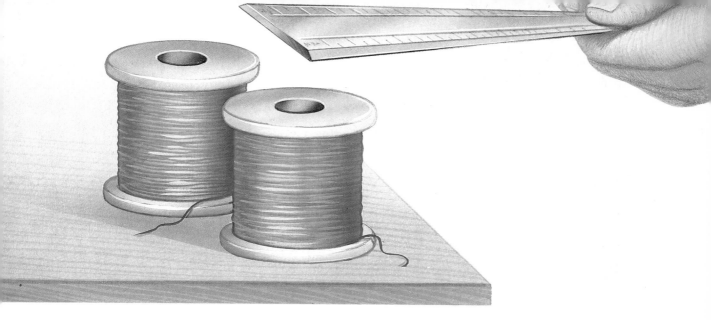

Line Your Eyes Up

1 You need two cotton reels or any two small objects that are the same and a ruler or other pointer.

2 Put the cotton reels on a table at eye level, one a little way behind the other.

3 Line them up with your eyes, then cover each eye in turn. Do they jump out of line?

4 Try to touch the back one with the ruler, first with both eyes open, then with one eye covered.

perfectly. They have to wear glasses to help them see. Imagine what it would be like if you could hardly see. Imagine what it would be like if you could not see at all.

Blind people use their other senses more than people who have sight, but nothing makes up for the loss of sight.

Does the cheese have a wedge cut out, or is an extra piece about to fall off the top?

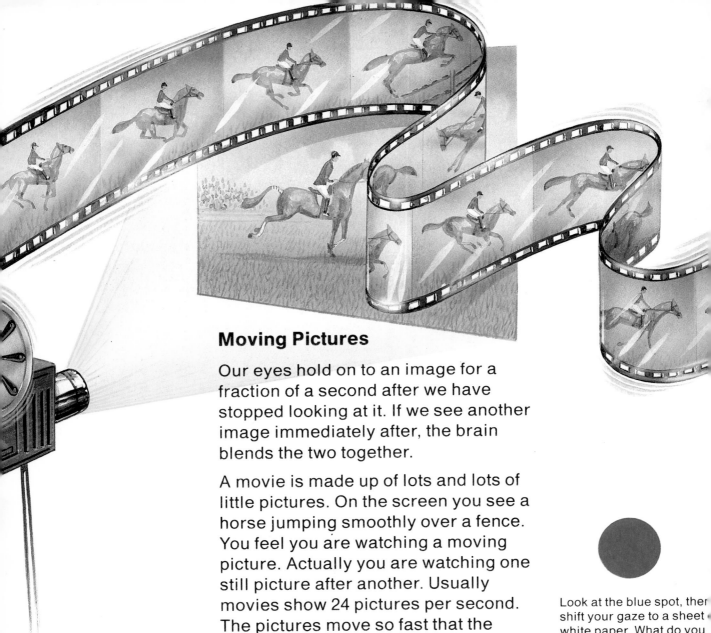

Moving Pictures

Our eyes hold on to an image for a
fraction of a second after we have
stopped looking at it. If we see another
image immediately after, the brain
blends the two together.

A movie is made up of lots and lots of
little pictures. On the screen you see a
horse jumping smoothly over a fence.
You feel you are watching a moving
picture. Actually you are watching one
still picture after another. Usually
movies show 24 pictures per second.
The pictures move so fast that the
image seems to be moving.

Look at the blue spot, then
shift your gaze to a sheet
white paper. What do you
see?

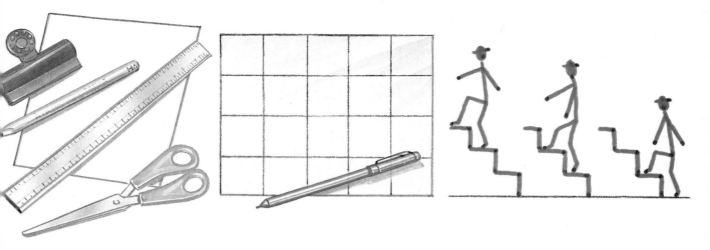

Make a Flicker Book

1 You need a sheet of thin white card, a ruler, a pencil, a pen or felt tip and a bulldog clip.

2 Rule 20 or 24 squares on the card.

3 Draw a pin man walking upstairs. You need him in three positions: once with a foot on each step, once with his back foot raised and once with his front foot raised.

4 Copy the picture several times in this order, putting one more step behind him and one more in front as you do it.

5 Cut the pictures out and stack them in order.

6 Grip one edge of the stack in a bulldog clip. Flick the other edge and watch the man walk upstairs as the pictures flash in front of your eyes.

13

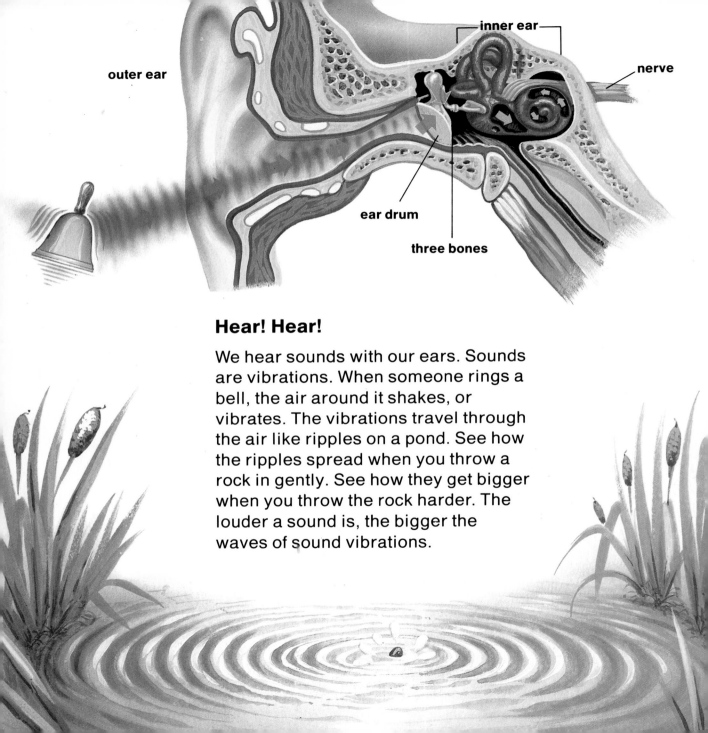

outer ear

inner ear

nerve

ear drum

three bones

Hear! Hear!

We hear sounds with our ears. Sounds are vibrations. When someone rings a bell, the air around it shakes, or vibrates. The vibrations travel through the air like ripples on a pond. See how the ripples spread when you throw a rock in gently. See how they get bigger when you throw the rock harder. The louder a sound is, the bigger the waves of sound vibrations.

Our ears pick up the vibrations and pass signals about them to our brain. Inside each ear we have an ear drum, which is like the skin of a real drum. When a wave of sound hits it, the ear drum vibrates. It makes three little bones next to it vibrate. They pass the vibrations on to the inner ear.

The inner ear is a coiled tube filled with liquid. Tiny hairs in the liquid pick up the vibrations. Nerves pass signals from them to the brain. The brain turns the signals into sounds.

Make a Set of Drums

1 You need some empty cans and containers with lids, some dry rice and a "drum stick".

2 Sprinkle some rice on each of the lids.

3 Tap the containers with your drum stick and watch the rice dance. When you hit a drum, vibrations travel through the lid and through the air. When you hit one drum, what happens to the rice on the others?

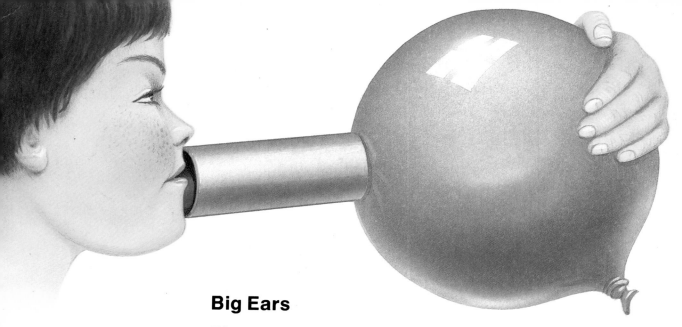

Big Ears

Blow up a balloon and see if you can feel the sound vibrations. Hold a tube of cardboard against the balloon and make a loud noise into it. Can you feel the vibrations in the skin of the balloon? Your ear drum feels sound vibrations in the same way.

The bones in your ears feel the vibrations too. You can feel sound travel through other bones in your body. Tap a kitchen fork and hold it to your ear. You can hear the sound of the prongs vibrating. While it still sounds bite the handle with your teeth. Does it sound louder?

Have you noticed how a dog pricks up its ears when it is listening? Without knowing it, the dog is trying to catch more vibrations. Most people cannot move their ears. They cup their hands behind their ears when they want to hear better. Try it with a ticking watch and hear the difference it makes.

You can collect even more vibrations with a funnel. Before hearing aids were invented, people used ear trumpets to help them hear better. You can make a paper ear trumpet by twisting paper into a cone. Hold the narrow end against your ear. Can you hear more? The more sound waves you collect, the better you hear.

What a Noise!

You need two ears for much the same reason that you need two eyes. With only one ear, it is hard to know where a sound is coming from. Get a friend to hide a ticking clock. Cover one ear and try to find it. Then try with both ears. Is it easier?

Oven Rack Chimes

1 You need an oven rack, some string and some "drum sticks"

2 Tie a length of string to each end of the rack.

3 Wind the string round your index fingers and put your fingers in your ears.

4 Get a friend to tap the bars of the rack. Listen to the sound as it travels up the string, through your fingers and into your ears.

5 Take one hand away from your ear and hold the rack with it. Get your friend to tap the bars again. Can you hear the difference?

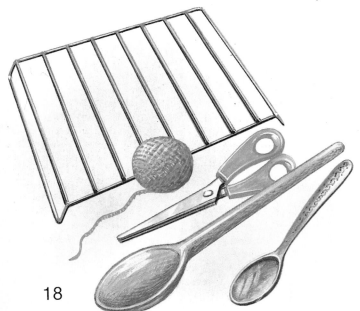

18

What is the worst sound you know?
Chalk scratching on a blackboard?
Jackhammers drilling? Fireworks
going bang? Can you think why there
are some nice sounds and some nasty
ones?

We call sounds that we do not like
noise. Nice sounds are smooth. Nasty
sounds are irritating because they are
not smooth. The nerves send signals to
the brain that we are hearing harmful
sounds. The irritation we feel warns us
to stop listening and protect our ears.

Some loud noises are even painful.
Loud or irritating noise can damage
your ears or make you deaf. Always
take care of your ears.

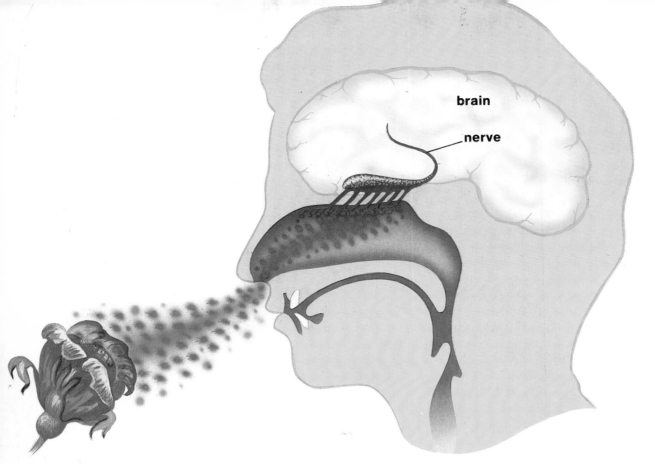

brain

nerve

skunk

Your Nose Knows

What is your favorite smell? Fried
onions? Ice cream with hot chocolate
sauce? Hot dogs? Roses? Do you feel
hungry when you can smell food
cooking? Do you feel nauseous and
hurry away from certain smells?

20

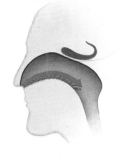

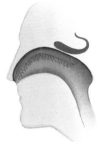

Sniff, Sniff

When you sniff, you force the air up against the sticky patch in your nose.

Smells are tiny particles that break off the surface of things and float in the air.

Inside your nose there is a sticky area covered with hairs. When you breathe in, air goes into your nose together with particles from all the objects around you. The particles are trapped by the hairs in your nose and dissolve in the sticky liquid. Nerves linked to the hairs send signals to your brain. It tells you what you are smelling.

Your sense of smell warns you when things are bad or dangerous. Bad foods and poisons mostly smell horrible. Animals use smell to find food, to find their way and to find a mate. The skunk uses smell to drive away its enemies.

What's that smell?

Get some smelly and some not so smelly foods from the kitchen cupboard. Blindfold your friends and see if they can guess what they are sniffing.

Tasty Tongue

Stick your tongue out at yourself in the mirror. What do you see? Your tongue is covered with tiny bumps called taste buds. Nerves inside your tongue link your taste buds to your brain. It tells you what you are tasting.

See what your taste buds can taste with this experiment.

Make a Map of Your Tongue

1 You need a sheet of paper, a pencil, four colored pencils, four cotton buds and four saucers of water. To mix with the water you need some salt, vinegar, sugar and instant coffee.

2 Draw an outline of your tongue and draw a grid over it.

3 In separate saucers, mix the sugar, salt, vinegar and coffee with just enough water to dissolve them.

4 Dip cotton buds into each saucer and test each area of your tougue with each of the flavors.

5 Mark on your map where you tasted each flavor most. Did the coffee taste more bitter on the tip of your tongue or at the back of your tongue?

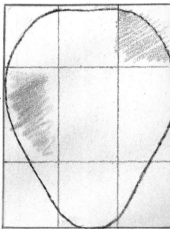

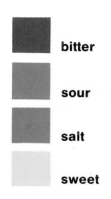

bitter

sour

salt

sweet

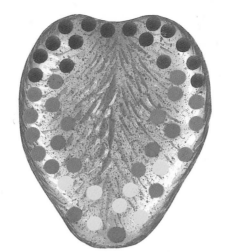

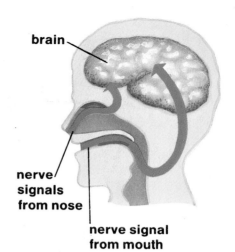

brain

nerve signals from nose

nerve signal from mouth

What's That Taste?

Can you taste the difference between tea and coffee? Put a drop of cooking oil in a cup of each. The film of oil on the surface prevents scented particles escaping, so your nose will be no help to you.

Our tongues can detect only four tastes. Salt, sweet, sour and bitter. The buds for each taste are on different parts of the tongue. Did your map of each taste come out like ours?

You can "taste" many different flavors because your sense of taste mixes with your sense of smell. When you have a cold, you cannot taste your food because your nose is blocked.

The spit, or saliva, in your mouth dissolves your food before you can taste it. Dab your tongue dry with a tissue and taste a few grains of sugar. Then sip some water to make the saliva flow. Is it sweeter now? Do the same thing with some salt and some coffee.

Not After That!

Do you like fries? Do you like strawberries? Do you like fries before or after your strawberries? Why do you think the order you eat things in matters?

23

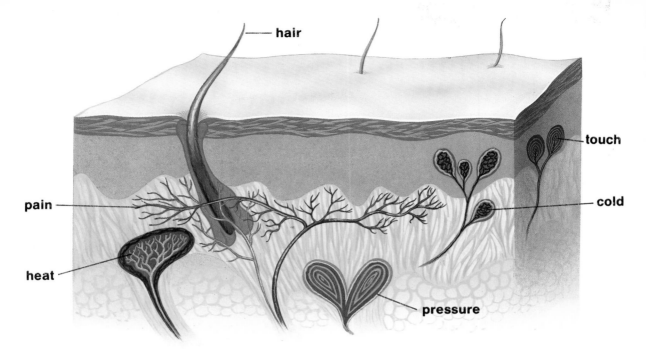

A Ticklish Business

Your skin is the largest sense organ of all. Tiny nerves all over your body send messages to your brain every time you touch or feel something. Some parts of your body have many more nerves than others. They are more sensitive.

Different nerves sense different things. Your skin can feel touch, heat, cold, pressure (squeezing) and pain.

Prickly plants and hairy caterpillars protect themselves by causing pain or irritation to people who touch them.

Test Your Hands

1 You need some sticky thread, some hot water, a spoon, some ice and a blunt pin.

2 Touch each part of your hand, front and back, with four things – the thread, the spoon after pressing it against the ice cube, the spoon after being dipped in hot water, and the pin.

3 Which part of your hand was most ticklish? Which disliked the cold most? Which could bear the most heat? Which felt the pin most often?

Which is more sensitive? The tip of your tongue or your big toe? Your face or the back of your head? The back of your neck or the front?

Does it Tickle?

1 You need a friend, a piece of paper, a pencil and one colored pencil.

2 Draw an outline of your friend's body on the paper.

3 Tickle different parts of your friend's body. Be gentle – your turn will be next. Never tickle anyone after they have asked you to stop.

4 Mark the areas that are most sensitive on your plan. Can you think why those parts are so sensitive?

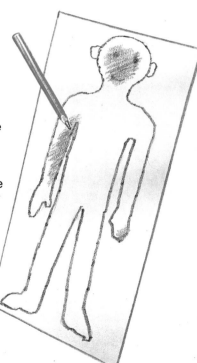

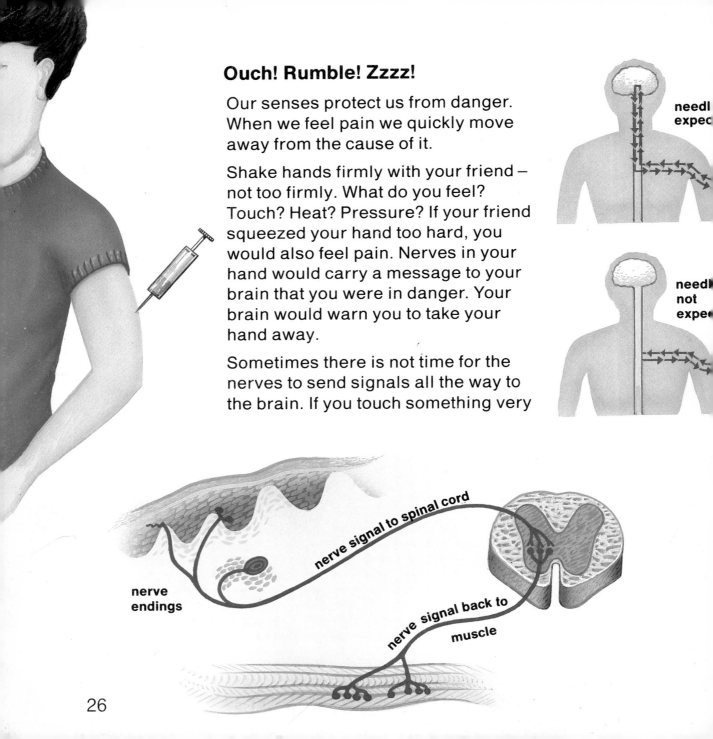

Ouch! Rumble! Zzzz!

Our senses protect us from danger. When we feel pain we quickly move away from the cause of it.

Shake hands firmly with your friend – not too firmly. What do you feel? Touch? Heat? Pressure? If your friend squeezed your hand too hard, you would also feel pain. Nerves in your hand would carry a message to your brain that you were in danger. Your brain would warn you to take your hand away.

Sometimes there is not time for the nerves to send signals all the way to the brain. If you touch something very

needl
exped

needl
not
exped

nerve
endings

nerve signal to spinal cord

nerve signal back to
muscle

hot, your hand jumps away before you know it. Your brain has not had time to tell you. The message has gone only as far as a nerve center in your spine which acts like your brain in an emergency.

If you know that someone is going to give you an injection, you do not jump away. Your brain tells you that the pain is not harmful. If someone pricks you without warning, you jump away before you have had time to think.

We can sense pain from deep inside our bodies. We can also sense when we feel hungry, thirsty or tired. Your brain tells you when you need to eat and drink, when you need to go to the toilet and when you need to go to sleep. Imagine what life would be like if you did not have pain and these other senses to keep you from harm.

Hoppity Floppity

Try standing on one foot with your eyes shut. Is it easy or do you wobble?

Which Way Up?

Stay quite still as you read this. Without looking, can you say what position your legs are in? Where are your feet? You do not have to look. Nerves in your muscles and joints send signals to your brain all the time telling you where they are.

Your brain sends signals back to the muscles and joints telling them when to stay still and when to move. You can make most movements without thinking. You never have to think when you walk or run or when you eat your food. Do you find hopping as easy?

inner
ear

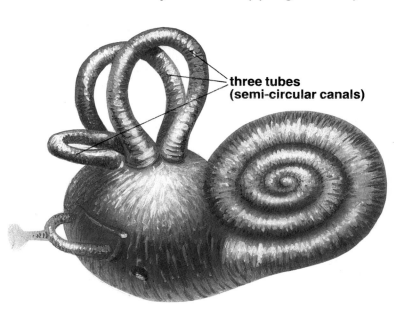

three tubes
(semi-circular canals)

inside tubes

28

Giddy Peas

Put some peas in a bowl of water. Swirl the bowl round and round. Then suddenly stop. See how the water carries on spinning like the liquid in your ears.

Spin round and round and then stop. Does the ground seem to go on spinning? Do you feel giddy? If you do, it is because you have upset your ears. As well as helping you hear, your ears help you balance.

Inside each of your ears is a set of tubes lined with tiny hairs. The tubes contain liquid full of little bits of grit. Nerves link the hairs to your brain. When you move, the liquid moves, too. Bits of grit brush against the hairs. Nerve signals tell your brain what position your head is in.

Test Your Senses

You cannot always believe what you see or hear. Often our senses seem to play tricks on us. Try these tricks with some of your friends.

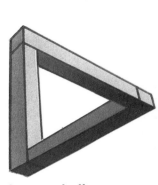

Can you eat with a knife and fork?

Everyone can use a knife and fork. Can you eat with them in opposite hands? Be careful if you try it.

Can you tell an apple from a potato?

Cut a piece of raw apple and a piece of raw potato to roughly the same size. Close your eyes, pinch your nose and taste each one. Can you tell the difference?

Can you believe your eyes?

Could you make this triangle out of wood or would it be impossible?

Can you see a white triangle?

There isn't one in the picture. There are only V-shapes and parts of circles.

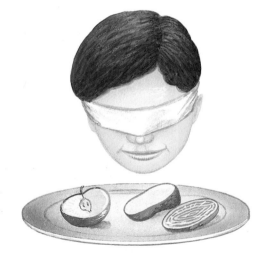

Can you put your fingers together?

Hold your hands out in front of you and touch your two first fingers together. Easy, isn't it? Try doing it with your arms raised above your head.

Can you tell an apple from a pear?

Cut a piece of each and taste them. There is no mistaking the flavor. Put a piece of cut onion under your nose and taste them again. Do they taste different now?

Is the water hot or cold?

Put some ice in a glass and fill it with cold water. Fill another glass with cold tap water. Fill another with hot tap water. Pick up the icy glass with one hand and the hot one with the other. Put them down and pick up the third glass with both hands. How does it feel? Is it warm or cool?

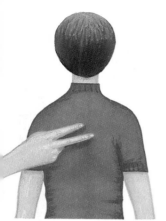

How many fingers

Touch your friend's back with one, two or three fingers. Ask each time how many there were. You can see from the number of wrong answers how few nerves you have in your back.

Are you wet or dry?

Put on rubber gloves. Dip your hands in ice-cold water, then put them in warm water. Did they feel wet in the cold water? The feeling of wetness is a mixture of coldness and pressure. Your hands feel wet even though you know your gloves are keeping them dry.

Can you rub your stomach and pat your head?

Start by patting the top of your head. Keep on patting and then rub your stomach round and round at the same time as if you felt nice and full. Try not to laugh!

Index and glossary